SEE AMERICAN HISTORY

WORLD WAR II
1939–1945

The Art of
MORT KÜNSTLER

Text by
JAMES I. ROBERTSON, JR.

★

ABBEVILLE KIDS
A DIVISION OF ABBEVILLE PRESS
New York   London

D1379856

In memory of the many teachers who
encouraged my interest in art. —MK

Front and back cover: *The F6F Hellcat fighter.* See page 39.
Front endpaper: Map of the European theater of World War II.
Back endpaper: Map of the Pacific theater of World War II.

Editor: Nicole Lanctot
Series design: Misha Beletsky
Composition: Ada Rodriguez
Production manager: Louise Kurtz

First edition
1 3 5 7 9 10 8 6 4 2

ISBN 978-0-7892-1261-0

Library of Congress Cataloging-in-Publication Data available upon request

For bulk or premium sales and for text adoption procedures, write to Customer Service
Manager, 116 West 23rd Street, New York, NY 10011, or call 1-800-ARTBOOK.
Visit Abbeville Press online at www.abbeville.com.

TABLE OF CONTENTS

The Story of World War II

World War II was a fight-to-the-death between democracy and dictatorship. In the 1930s three nations with the strong will to expand their reach — Germany, Italy, and Japan — began pushing into neighboring countries until other nations finally pushed back.

In Germany, the Nazi party leader Adolf Hitler came to power and began expanding his nation's territory into other countries of central Europe. When he led Germany, he held great rallies for his supporters and inflamed them with ideas that certain people did not have a right to exist on earth. The Holocaust — the mass slaughter of the Jewish people and other civilians — was the direct result.

In 1940 the three governments of Germany, Italy, and Japan formed an alliance known as the Axis powers. The leader of the Soviet Union, Joseph Stalin, also sided with Hitler, at least to begin with.

Things first changed when Germany invaded Poland. It had just gone too far. Both France and Great Britain declared war on Germany. As German soldiers advanced into France, a new prime minister took over in London, one who would show an iron will to contain the Axis: Winston Churchill. Meanwhile, Japan decided to challenge the United States in the Pacific by attacking Pearl Harbor. This aggressive act shocked the Americans out of their neutrality under the leadership of President Franklin Roosevelt. When Hitler's plans to invade Soviet territory were revealed, Stalin changed sides. The independent government of China allied itself with this coalition, too. The new group would fight together as the Allied powers.

The struggle would last six years and a day (September 1, 1939, to September 2, 1945) and produce the largest armies and most horrible weapons ever created. Thirty countries would battle on the continents of Europe, Africa, and Asia and over great stretches of the Atlantic and Pacific Oceans and all of the Mediterranean Sea. It left 50 million people dead and much of the world in ruins.

More aircraft combat occurred than had ever been seen before. U.S. factories turned out 230,000 aircraft so fast it seemed as if the paint would still be wet when the planes went into action. Although some aircraft had been used in World War I, in World War II they were everywhere. They were sent on bombing runs and to defend against enemy bombers. The Battle of Britain was an extended air attack by the Germans. They transported vital supplies. Aircraft carriers for the first time took planes close to the action and were critical in the Pacific.

In 1942 U.S. and British infantry combat troops drove the Germans and Italians from North Africa. Allied forces pushed farther north to occupy Sicily and then onto the mainland. Advancing through "the boot" of Italy, thousands of soldiers fought in dozens of major battles over the next two years until Rome fell to the Allies on June 4, 1944.

On June 6, 1944, the European war shifted to the French coast. In the largest land-sea operation in history, more than 100,000 soldiers fought to get an Allied foothold. The D-Day invasion met strong resistance from the Germans. But Allied troops pushed their way through France, across Belgium, and finally into Germany. In December, a desperate German counterattack — the Battle of the Bulge — failed. Russian, British, and American forces advanced steadily toward the German capital of Berlin. Hitler committed suicide rather than be captured. On May 8, 1945, Germany surrendered. Sadly, President Franklin Roosevelt had died of a stroke a month earlier.

A different war took place in the Pacific because of the different geography. Campaigns were fought more on water than on land, and U.S. forces were mostly on their own. From 1942 to 1945, aircraft carriers, warships, submarines, and troop ships engaged in "island-hopping." Each small target was one more important stretch of land closer to Japan. Little islands with unfamiliar names became unforgettable battlefields: Guadalcanal, Attu, Kiska, Guam, Iwo Jima, Saipan, and Okinawa. Some of the greatest naval battles in history were fought at Coral Sea, Midway, and Leyte Gulf. Americans won those naval fights with aircraft, not the heavy guns of warships.

In the fierce conflicts of the Pacific the cost in human life was high. Still, the American military was steadily closing in on Japan itself, but everyone knew that taking the islands of Japan would mean countless more would die on both sides. When the Japanese refused to surrender, the new U.S. president Harry Truman turned to the secret weapon scientists had been working on for five years: the atomic bomb. It would have the explosive force of 2,000 bombers carrying standard missiles.

Two atomic bombs, or "A-bombs," were dropped on the Japanese cities of Hiroshima and Nagasaki on August 6 and August 9 in 1945. Each disappeared in a blinding flash of blazing heat that created winds in excess of 650 miles per hour. The Japanese government promptly surrendered, and the war formally ended on September 2, 1945.

The Battle of Britain

★1940

Under Adolf Hitler, the Nazi war machine at first seemed unstoppable.
German troops invaded Poland, Denmark, Norway, Belgium, and the
Netherlands—all in a matter of months. Only England held fast in
Western Europe.

Across the Atlantic, the United States remained officially neutral
in the war. However, President Franklin Roosevelt had begun basic

military preparations. One step was to call up members of the National Guard for active duty. The part-time militia from Oklahoma left happily for what they thought would be a one-year tour of duty. In this painting (LEFT) families are saying good-bye to soldiers leaving for war. It would be *five years* before those who survived would return home.

Hitler sought to conquer England through airpower. From July to October of 1940, thousands of German bombers blasted English cities, airfields, and industrial plants. Royal Air Force pilots, flying Spitfire (BELOW) and Hurricane fighters, were outnumbered but stubbornly brave. They destroyed 1,900 German aircraft before the country's plans for invading England were abandoned. This Battle of Britain was the first major defeat of German military forces. Prime Minister Winston Churchill would say of his British airmen's success: "Never in the field of human conflict was so much owed by so many to so few."

Pearl Harbor: A Sleeping Giant Awakens

★1941

It happened without warning. Just after dawn on Sunday, December 7, 1941, some 350 Japanese planes attacked Pearl Harbor in the Hawaiian Islands. It was the largest naval base the United States had in the

Pacific Ocean. The Japanese bombers, torpedo planes, and fighters (FAR LEFT), launched from six aircraft carriers, struck in two waves. See the torpedo plane flying low above the water?

What resulted has been called "the most costly defeat ever suffered by the United States." All eight U.S. battleships were sunk or heavily damaged. Three cruisers and three destroyers were reduced to smoke and flames. Nearly 190 airplanes sitting on the ground were destroyed. Over 3,500 Americans would be killed or wounded.

The Japanese admiral in charge of the attack commented sadly the next day: "I fear all we have done is awaken a sleeping giant and fill him with a terrible resolve." An angry President Franklin Roosevelt (ABOVE) asked Congress to declare war on Japan, Germany, and Italy. Five months after Pearl Harbor, American forces pulled a surprise of their own. Sixteen B-25 Mitchell medium-sized bombers (BELOW) took

off from the aircraft carrier *Hornet.* Flying just above the water and in single file to avoid detection, the squadron traveled 600 miles and bombed the Japanese capital of Tokyo. Many of the airmen shouted America's new battle cry: "Remember Pearl Harbor!"

In the Asian Jungles

★1942

President Roosevelt put Gen. Joseph Stilwell in charge of the military operations in China, Burma, and India. He had two duties: to block a Japanese invasion of India and to keep the Burma Road open. The winding dirt highway was China's only lifeline with the outside world. It zigzagged 140 miles through jungles and over mountains.

Stilwell had such a sour personality that his men called him "Vinegar Joe." Still he marched and fought beside his troops. His force was not large enough to launch attacks, but Stilwell fought a number of successful battles over a two-year period.

For air support, the general depended on a handful of rather old P-40 Flying Tiger fighters. In Asia the P-40 was best known for the tiger shark's head painted on its nose (ABOVE). See the plane escaping the flames?

In this picture of Stilwell (LEFT), the general marches confidently ahead of his troops, wearing a large ammunition belt. If you look closely, you can see a hand grenade on his left shoulder. A grenade becomes active by pulling the pin, then quickly throwing it at an enemy before it explodes. Dangerous work!

America's First Invasion

In order to defeat Japan, U.S. forces first needed to get control of "key" islands that Japan occupied spread out across the western Pacific Ocean. Each island the U.S. soldiers took would bring the Americans closer to the enemy's home base.

When the American troops captured an island, most of the time they built airstrips. U.S. bombers could then "leapfrog" shorter distances and have more time in the sky.

This approach started in August 1942. The Japanese were building an air base on the island of Guadalcanal to make it easier to bombard Allied ships steaming to and from Australia. Over 10,000 marines stormed ashore in the first invasion of Japanese-held territory. In both paintings (LEFT and BELOW), American soldiers combat enemy soldiers from Japan, which sent some of its best troops to defend the island.

Fighting lasted eleven months. Soldiers struggled through dense thickets and rain forest. On occasion, Japanese soldiers made suicide attacks on American positions. These were called *banzai* attacks because this is what the Japanese soldiers shouted when they charged. Temperatures regularly soared above 100 degrees, and the Marines also suffered from several jungle diseases, notably malaria. Yet Americans eventually forced the surviving Japanese to abandon the island.

Guadalcanal was the first major land victory in the Pacific. It was the starting point for three years of successful invasions of the territories surrounding the islands of Japan.

The War at Sea

★1942

Airpower was the key to victory in the Pacific operations. The large navies provided heavy-gun support during invasions and kept enemy vessels at a distance. But World War II demonstrated that a battleship's big 16-inch guns were no match for planes dropping bombs and torpedoes. Crew members on a ship's deck were easy targets for gunfire from fighter aircraft. Aircraft carriers would replace battleships as the central pieces of a naval fleet.

One of the American ships at Guadalcanal was the cruiser *Chicago*. (Cruisers were second in size only to battleships. Battleships are named for states, while cruisers are named after cities.) *Chicago* had been hit by two torpedoes and was being towed away for repairs. Japanese fighter-bombers broke through the cover of American F4F Wildcats (ABOVE), which were no match for the Japanese Zero fighters.

In this painting (LEFT), one plane is making a deadly dive into the cruiser. Four torpedoes have already torn gaping holes in the ship. Look in the upper right-hand corner of this scene. Despite all of the shooting and explosions, a small crew is working dutifully to put out one of the many fires.

Wolves Underwater

★1940–1944

Germany built the first large fleet of submarines. These U-boats patrolled the Atlantic Ocean. They operated individually or as a team (a "wolfpack").

Their weapon was the torpedo: a self-propelled missile that sped beneath the surface and exploded on contact. Between July and October, 1940, German submarines sank 217 ships.

Their successes faded when the United States entered the war. American planes and ships proved to be good sub hunters, as seen in the painting (BELOW). When Germany did not replace lost underwater vessels, it gave the Allies the upper hand in submarine warfare.

In the Pacific, U.S. subs also sank 1,042 Japanese ships (ABOVE), which was half of that nation's life-supporting merchant fleet.

Working in a submarine was not pleasant. There was very little space to move around in, and long periods passed without going to the water surface to get fresh air. It was also the most dangerous of naval duties. The U.S. Navy only accepted volunteers for the "silent service." Although these vessels traveled underwater and struck quickly, they could be helpless if the enemy pinpointed their position with electronic gear or bombs from low-flying aircraft. Even when a submarine was under attack, its crew could only sit helplessly and wait.

Skies over Europe

The best-known airplane in World War II was the B-17 Flying Fortress (BELOW). It dominated high-altitude bombing. It was built to fly high

and fast, and to defend itself better than any other plane ever has. It carried thirteen machine guns in front, rear, top, bottom, and on either side. The turrets on top and bottom could turn in a complete circle.

A normal bomb load was 5,000 pounds, but a Flying Fortress could carry three times that amount if necessary. What made this plane so feared was its now-famous Norden "bombsight." The instrument was so accurate, one pilot said, that he could "drop a bomb into a pickle barrel."

For a concentrated bomb run, B-17s sometimes flew in tight formations with up to twenty-eight planes grouped together. German fighters were known to fly above such wing-to-wing aircraft and drop bombs in an effort to shoot them down.

Less successful as a heavy bomber was the high-winged B-24 Liberator. The low point in its history came in 1943, when 178 of the bombers flew from Benghazi in North Africa and bombed oil fields in Ploeşti, Romania (ABOVE RIGHT) that supplied Germany. The Germans found out ahead of time that the bombers were coming, and they were ready for a powerful counterattack of antiaircraft fire. Only thirteen of the Liberator planes returned from the mission.

From Africa to Italy

Eleven months after Pearl Harbor, the first U.S. soldiers saw action against the Germans. These GIs joined British forces in North Africa against German and Italian armies.

From there, the Allies seized Sicily in the Mediterranean Sea and then invaded Italy. Fighting in this Axis country was vicious (see the bigger painting, LEFT), and casualties on both sides were high. It took two years of combat spread over cities, farmlands, and mountains before Italy fell to American-British forces.

GIs were not professional soldiers. They were volunteers and citizens called to the military and then highly trained. They wore in battle a simple "fatigue" suit rather than a tailored uniform. The three-pound steel helmet they wore was never comfortable, but it could usually stop a bullet. The American infantry pictured (BELOW) are carrying the M1 carbine, the best shoulder-weapon in the war. Officers—such as the soldier on the very far left—often had pistols strapped to their waists.

U.S. proved to be among "the best of the best." They did not want to fight—nobody likes to risk their lives. But they stepped forward to defend their country and the freedom of their allies, and they didn't want to let their comrades down.

Death Camps

★1939–1945

The worst evil of Nazi Germany was the Holocaust: an attempt to rid the world of all Jewish people. During the war years, six million Jewish men, women, and children were herded like livestock to more than thirty concentration camps in Germany and occupied countries. These clusters of heavily guarded wooden buildings were called work camps, but in reality they were death camps. The old, crippled, and very young were killed shortly after arrival. Beatings, starvation, and exposure to the elements were common. Those who were physically able to work were hired out as laborers and miners. When hunger, overwork, or illness left them too weak to keep up, they were packed in large rooms. The rooms would fill with poisonous gas, and everyone in them died.

Auschwitz in Germany was the most repulsive of the camps. An estimated three million helpless civilians died there at the hands of the Nazis. More than 35,000 Jews were executed at the Buchenwald compound. After the war, another 36,000 bodies were uncovered at Belsen. At one camp, excavators uncovered thousands of pairs of babies' shoes, which meant that even very small children were killed in large numbers. News about this discovery angered the world.

It was not only Jewish people who were sent to Hitler's death camps. Millions of Christians and Catholics from Poland, Hungary, Czechoslovakia, the Ukraine, Russia, Holland, France, and even Germany were taken from their homes and killed in concentration camps, too. These were immigrants, priests, the sick and disabled, and anyone who did not agree with German laws and Hitler's beliefs.

D-Day

★1944

June 6, 1944, was called "D-Day": the invasion of Nazi-held Europe. The location was the French coast, only twenty miles across the channel from England.

Allied warships first pounded the German coastal defenses with artillery. Bombers struck railroads, supply depots, highways, and fuel dumps behind the lines. Fighter planes, notably P-47 Thunderbolts and P-51 Mustangs, attacked gun stations along the shore. Parachuters jumped out of transport planes and gliders. But, as American infantrymen proudly say: "The last 100 yards belong to us."

Tens of thousands of foot soldiers came across the channel in small landing craft (LEFT). The assaults on the shore met a number of problems, as seen in the other painting (ABOVE). Choppy waters caused widespread seasickness. Some men jumped ashore too quickly and drowned in deep water. Heavy machinery bogged down in wet sand. Bombers missed their coastal targets, and the German fire was heavier than Allied soldiers had ever seen.

Losses climbed sharply in the day-by-day intense combat. Landing troops slowly fortified the area around the Allied beachhead, and the forces were able to spread forward. By the end of June, the advance against German forces was well underway.

Battle of the Bulge

★1944

Freezing weather and sleet in mid-December brought a halt to the Allied advance. Units became scattered and isolated. German dictator Adolf Hitler bet everything on one last blow to these forces. He concentrated a large army and launched a surprise attack in the

snow-covered forests of Belgium. See the snowy trees and overcast sky behind the soldiers (LEFT)? Fog also hid every movement.

It was a fight between some of Germany's best soldiers and the United States's most seasoned veterans. The Germans advanced fifty miles in ten days. The American line bent, but it would not break in this "Battle of the Bulge." Early in the fighting, a German commander demanded that America surrender. Gen. Anthony McAuliffe of the 101st Airborne Division only replied "Nuts!" and continued to resist.

By Christmas, the weather improved. Lines of Sherman tanks rushed to the aid of soldiers pinned down at the town of Bastogne. This was the largest battle fought on the Western Front in World War II. Some one million soldiers were involved, and 120,000 were killed, wounded, or captured. This was also the last major Nazi offensive.

Look at the tank commander (ABOVE). He is using his radio to give commands to other tanks. To his left is a heavy-caliber machine gun to use against infantry, while the tank fires from its 75-mm cannon.

Underground Operations

★1940–1945

In 1939 and 1940 German troops occupied several nations, including France. But they learned painfully that while they controlled the land and the government, they could not break the spirit of the people. Many civilians were willing to fight behind the lines individually or in small groups. They were called "resistance fighters," "partisans," and "the underground movement." Every participant understood that if he or she were captured, instant death would follow.

French guerrillas used every form of damage (also known as "sabotage") that would aid the Allied cause. They ambushed German troops, wrecked trains, blew up bridges, and raided supply depots. In addition, they provided information on German activities—usually by using shortwave radios. When Allied pilots were shot down, or when parachutists were blown off course from their landing point, the partisans were truly lifesavers.

Naturally, these resistance fighters did not wear uniforms. Trust and the belief that the Nazi occupation was wrong were the links that held them together. At public events, they knew they could do an act of sabotage, then disappear into the crowd without anyone pointing them out. They were a brave "second army" to the Allied forces in Europe. They cannot be seen in this painting of the German surrender in France (BELOW), but they had helped a great deal to gain that hard-earned victory.

Control of the Pacific
★1942–1945

In Europe, U.S. soldiers fought against people with a culture and habits that were familiar to them in a traditional land war. In the Pacific, things were different. There, American forces battled for islands hundreds of miles from one another. The residents were people who spoke no English and had a very different culture, and they were wary of these invaders from the West.

In this painting (LEFT), Marines move through an island village cautiously.

The marine in front has a hand grenade within easy reach. His weapon is the BAR, the Browning automatic rifle. It was larger and weighed more than the M1 carbine that the second marine is carrying. The carbine fired a 30-caliber bullet and was accurate to 300 yards. The weapon did not have to be cocked after each firing; one simply pulled the trigger and the firing began.

Basic training had given these men a close bond with one another. They were "brothers all," whether in camp or facing death in a sinking ship. You can see that the "Abandon Ship!" order was issued after torpedoes from a Japanese submarine hit a U.S. naval vessel (ABOVE).

Sinking of the *Yamato*

★1945

The Imperial Japanese Navy had never suffered a defeat prior to World War II. But staggering blows delivered by U.S. ships and carrier-based planes soon left Japan with only a handful of major warships. One was the *Yamato*, the flagship of the Japanese fleet and the largest battleship ever constructed. Weighing 73,000 tons, *Yamato* towered over all other vessels at sea. It had nine 18-inch guns, the largest ever fitted on a ship. Twelve other cannon in three turrets gave it a firing power no other battleship could match.

In April 1945, the *Yamato* (the big ship in the painting, LEFT) steamed toward a confrontation at Okinawa with eight destroyers and a cruiser as a naval escort. However, no air cover was available, and U.S. pilots easily spotted the battleship. More than 100 aircraft bombed and torpedoed the naval giant. For two hours the *Yamato* was pounded until it sank with an immense loss of life.

The huge warship never had a chance to fire its great guns against opposing naval vessels. Its loss was a sign that the centuries-old battleship era was past.

The U.S. conquest of the Pacific islands (see the fighting, BELOW) took over a year, beginning with marines landing in Saipan in June 1944 and ending with the liberation of the Philippine Islands in July 1945.

Island Hopping

★1945

In the spring of 1945, combined U.S. sea and land forces delivered a final one-two punch against the Japanese. Marines struck the volcanic island of Iwo Jima, where the enemy had an airstrip and radar warning station. Two months later, a large army-marine force went ashore at Okinawa, a large island only 325 miles from Japan. An excellent harbor made Okinawa an ideal jumping-off point for invading Japan itself.

At Iwo Jima, Americans found 20,000 Japanese soldiers defending only eight square miles of land. U.S. troops used flamethrowers, hand grenades, and tanks to take the island foot by foot over a period of four months. Early in the action, Americans raised the Stars and Stripes atop Iwo Jima's mountain (LEFT). A photographer captured the moment, and it lives on in this painting and in a bronze monument in Washington, D.C.

Okinawa proved even tougher to conquer. Japanese troops defended the island in force, along with many natives who had been told that the Americans were coming to kill them. Some of the most intense fighting of the entire war took place there, shown in this painting (ABOVE). In the end, 110,000 Japanese were killed and 11,000 captured. The United States lost 7,600 in the land fighting.

Kamikazes

★1945

At Okinawa the U.S. Navy suffered 5,000 casualties in offshore action. Most of those deaths were the result of suicide attacks from the air. The pilots who made these deadly runs were called *kamikazes* (a Japanese word meaning "divine wind"). They loaded outdated airplanes with 500-pound bombs. Teenagers were taught just enough flying lessons to get their planes to the American fleet and then to dive into warships. These young and inexperienced airmen seemed quite willing to kill themselves.

This type of fighting was something Americans had not seen before. Japanese pilots saw this type of death as honorable—an ultimate sacrifice as U.S. forces were closing in on their homeland—while American soldiers wanted to make it out alive.

During the Okinawa campaign, kamikazes made their greatest impact. Kamikazes at Okinawa encountered the F6F Hellcat fighter (BELOW), a vastly better plane than the old F4F Wildcat in use earlier in the war. Even so, Japanese pilots sank twenty-nine American ships and put sixty others out of commission. A total of 135 planes attacked the U.S. fleet. In this painting (LEFT), two Japanese fighter-bombers are heading for the already-damaged flight deck of the USS *Saratoga*. A third plane, in the lower left corner, has just missed the target. *Saratoga* survived the attack and slowly made it back to Pearl Harbor, but its fighting days were over.

A Unique Fighter Plane

Aircraft first became a military weapon in World War I, but it was in World War II that aerial combat played a dominant role. Every nation had well-known planes patrolling the skies, such as the British Spitfire. The United States produced a number of outstanding aircraft. The best of the fighter-bombers was certainly the F4U Corsair (ABOVE).

   It was originally designed to operate from aircraft carriers. However, the Corsair proved better as a land-based plane providing

support for ground troops. Most of the time marines were their pilots.

Everything about the Corsair was big. Its engine was the largest available at the time. The wings were gull shaped to make room for longer propellers. The plane was the first fighter able to fly comfortably at over 400 miles per hour. Six machine guns were mounted in the wings. The plane could also carry up to 4,000 pounds of bombs.

The "Bent Wing Exterminator" (one of its nicknames) won lasting fame for successful combat at Iwo Jima and Okinawa. When in a diving attack, the Corsair gave off a loud, shrill noise. Japanese troops gave the Corsair another nickname: "Whistling Death."

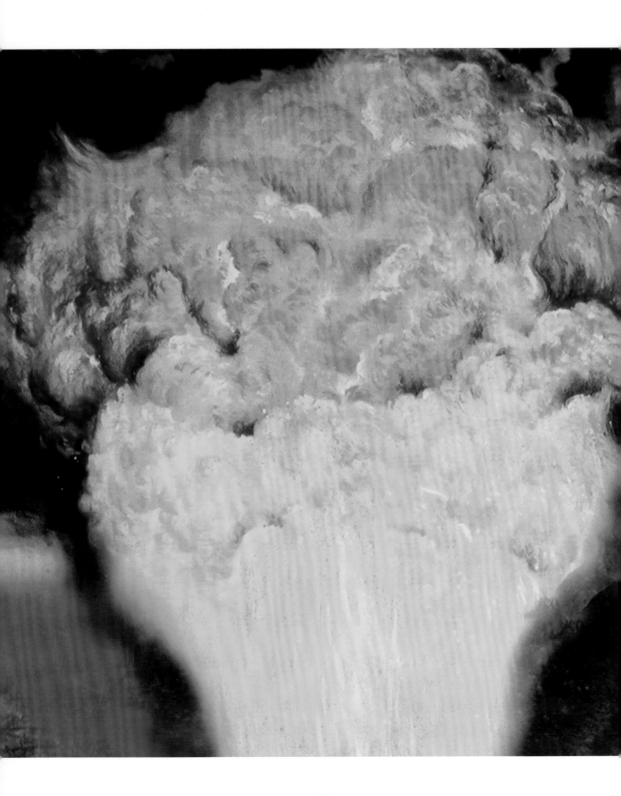

Atomic Bombs

★1945

With Germany's surrender in May 1945, the only one of the Axis powers still fighting was Japan. The Japanese were refusing all demands for their surrender. By this time the United States had developed two atomic bombs with awesome destructive power. President Harry Truman saw that an invasion of Japan would mean many, many more deaths on both sides. He gave the order to use the A-bombs to hurry the end of the war.

On the morning of August 6, a bomb exploded 1,600 feet above the industrial city of Hiroshima. There was a blinding flash and a tremendous roar. An eyewitness wrote of "a wave of suffocating heat and a wind that swept away everything in its path." A huge, mushroom-shaped cloud billowed eight miles into the sky.

The center of Hiroshima was totally destroyed. Over 100,000 Japanese were killed instantly. A similar number later died of burns, radiation sickness, and associated illnesses.

Japanese leaders made no sign that they would now surrender, so three days later a B-29 dropped the second bomb on the seaport of Nagasaki. The result was the same. One official stated that it was "a zone of utter death in which nothing remained alive." Another 100,000 soldiers and civilians died from the explosion.

The next day the Japanese lobbied for peace. On September 2, 1945, the treaty was signed on board the USS *Missouri*, anchored in Tokyo Harbor. World War II was finally over. The painful and unforgettable era would now become part of history.

★ World War II: Timeline

1940

March 7: President Roosevelt orders Pacific fleet to concentrate at Pearl Harbor as a warning to Japan.

June 18: Germany begins four-month air bombardment of England.

September 27: Germany, Italy, and Japan sign treaty pledging to defend one another in war. The group is known as the Axis powers.

November 4: Roosevelt declares United States to be officially neutral. He added: "I cannot ask that every American remain neutral in thought as well."

November 5: Roosevelt wins unprecedented third term as president of the United States.

1941

June 22: In spite of peace treaty with Russia, Adolf Hitler orders a full-scale attack on the Soviet Union.

December 7: Japan bombs Pearl Harbor.

December 8: United States enters World War II on the Allied side.

1942

January 1: United Nations formed from twenty-six countries by then at war with Axis powers.

January 15: Japan invades Burma.

April 18: "Doolittle Raid" on Tokyo gives notice of American might in spite of earlier defeat.

May 6: The Philippines fall to Japan; "Death March" of U.S. prisoners follows.

May 7–8: U.S. naval fleet wins battle of Coral Sea.

June 3–6: Victory at Midway cripples Japanese fleet and marks turning point in Pacific war.

August 7: Marines invade Guadalcanal and will take the island after a five-month campaign.

November 8: U.S. forces enter European war by first landing forces in North Africa.

1943

January 27: U.S. bombers make first air attack on targets inside Germany.

May 11-30: Americans drive Japanese from Aleutian Islands in Alaska.

July 10: Allies invade Sicily.

September 9: First U.S. troops land on Italian mainland.

1944

June 4: U.S. forces capture Rome, the capital of Italy.

June 6: D-Day invasion of France.

June 15: Marines land on Saipan to begin a month of fighting.

July 25: Allies begin powerful offensive through Belgium and France.

August 23: Paris is liberated from the Nazis.

September 11: American forces drive into Germany itself and push toward Berlin.

October 23: Largest naval battle of the war brings U.S. victory at Leyte Gulf.

December 16: "Battle of the Bulge" starts in Belgium.

1945

February 19: Marines storm ashore at Iwo Jima.

February 25: U.S. forces begin the final assault in Germany.

April 1: U.S. forces strike Okinawa and begin eighty-one days of air, naval, and land battles.

April 12: President Roosevelt dies of natural causes; Harry Truman becomes new U.S. president.

May 7: German surrender takes place in a modest schoolhouse.

August 6: Atomic bomb dropped on Hiroshima.

August 9: Second atomic bomb devastates Nagasaki.

September 2: Japan surrenders to Gen. Douglas MacArthur.

★ Key People

Bradley, Omar Nelson (1893–1981) This senior corps commander in Europe was the first Chairman of the Joint Chiefs of Staff and the last five-star general to die.

Churchill, Winston Leonard Spencer (1874–1965) Twice prime minister of the United Kingdom, "Winny" is the most quoted of all World War II leaders.

De Gaulle, Charles Andre Joseph Marie (1890–1970) This leader of the Free French during the war was later elected president of France.

Doolittle, James Harold (1896–1993) This major-general and commander of the Eighth Air Force is remembered most for leading the 1942 air strike against Tokyo.

Eisenhower, Dwight David (1890–1969) "Ike" was supreme commander of Allied forces in Europe and the invasions of North Africa, France, and Germany. He was elected thirty-fourth president of the United States.

Goebbels, Joseph (1897–1845) Minister of Propaganda in Nazi Germany, he was Hitler's closest advisor.

Göring, Hermann Wilhelm (1893–1946) This World War I pilot became head of Hitler's air force (the Luftwaffe). He committed suicide on the eve of his execution for war crimes.

Halsey, William Frederick, Jr. (1882–1959) Aggressive and prone to arguing, "Bull" Halsey was the fleet commander who won the naval battle of Leyte Gulf.

Himmler, Heinrich (1900–1945) One of Hitler's most powerful officers, Himmler was in charge of the concentration camps.

Hirohito (1901–1989) Even though he was emperor of Japan, military leaders turned him into a figurehead with little power.

Hitler, Adolf (1889–1945) As Chancellor of Germany, he is the man most responsible for World War II and the terrible loss of life and property that resulted.

Hull, Cordell (1871–1955) He served the longest tenure of any secretary of state in U.S. history and received the Nobel Peace Prize for helping to form the United Nations.

MacArthur, Douglas (1880–1964) He was the five-star general to command the Pacific theater.

Montgomery, Bernard (1887–1976) A brilliant field marshal in the British armies, he often argued with superiors—notably Eisenhower.

Murphy, Audie Leon (1925–1971). He received every military combat award for valor, including the Medal of Honor, and went on to be a successful movie star.

Mussolini, Benito (1883–1945) "Il Duce" was prime minister of Italy and head of its Fascist Party. He was deposed and killed by his own people late in the war.

Nimitz, Chester William (1885–1966) At the outset of the war, he was the nation's leading authority on submarines. His victory at Midway brought him international fame.

Patton, George Smith, Jr. (1885–1945) Probably World War II's most colorful figure, "Old Blood and Guts" wore pearl-handled pistols and employed tanks as if they were infantry units.

Rommel, Erwin (1891–1944) Germany's best general, he acquired the nickname "Desert Fox" for his skill in the 1942 North African campaign.

Roosevelt, Franklin Delano (1882–1945) "FDR" led the nation for twelve years through the Great Depression and a great world war. The Constitution now forbids a person from serving more than eight years as chief executive.

Stalin, Joseph (1879–1953) An early ally of Hitler, he then became a controversial partner in the Allied forces. He was known for his ruthlessness in cementing his control of Russia.

Tojo, Hideki (1884–1948) This general became prime minister of Japan and directed its wartime activities. He was arrested, condemned for war crimes, and hanged on December 23, 1948.

Truman, Harry S. (1884–1972): The thirty-third president of the United States, Truman completed the wartime duties at the death of FDR.

Yamamoto, Isoroku (1884–1943): As commander in chief of the Japanese navy, he was the person who planned and carried out the attack on Pearl Harbor. His death in a plane shot down by the Americans was a severe loss to Japanese naval operations.